CATS' TAILS FROM AMAZONIA

Sylvia Hobbs

ARTHUR H. STOCKWELL LTD
Torrs Park   Ilfracombe   Devon
Established 1898
www.ahstockwell.co.uk

© *Sylvia Hobbs, 2009*
First published in Great Britain, 2009
All rights reserved.
No part of this publication may be reproduced
or transmitted in any form or by any means,
electronic or mechanical, including photocopy,
recording, or any information storage and
retrieval system, without permission
in writing from the copyright holder.

British Library Cataloguing-in-Publication Data.
A catalogue record for this book is available
from the British Library.

Arthur H. Stockwell Ltd bears no responsibility
for the accuracy of events recorded in this book.

By the same author:
Alone in the Shadows

ISBN 978-0-7223-3933-6
Printed in Great Britain by
Arthur H. Stockwell Ltd
Torrs Park   Ilfracombe
Devon

Contents

Zara   5

Shadowlands   10

Pipkins   15

La Chambre sous la Cuisine pour les Chats   21

Zara
(My Story So Far)

Hi. I am Zara. Well, that is the name I have been given by my foster-mum.

Three weeks ago it was pouring with rain. It was a Thursday afternoon, and I found my little body becoming exceedingly wet and cold. I had been abandoned in a busy suburb of Bristol. A very noble gentleman working nearby spotted me on the edge of the pavement. His kindly hands clutched my little sodden body close to his open shirt. I heard his voice, and realised that I had been saved.

The kindness of this action gave me faith in humans again. The kind man dried my fur, and, still speaking softly to me, he took me home. His wife gave me a bowl of tuna and a drink of water.

Later that day – I believe it was about teatime – I was put into a pet carrier and driven, crying, to Amazonia. Well, I was glad to be in that heavenly cattery. A warm fleece was wrapped around my still slightly damp body, and a dish of delightful kitten

food was provided. I wolfed it down with some fresh, cool water.

Did I sleep? My word, I did! I was aware of company, but I was too weary to observe my new surroundings with any confidence. After all, I was only eight weeks old.

The following day, I was introduced to the other occupants at breakfast time. Our litter trays were cleaned thoroughly, our mats were brushed, and our blankets were shaken and tidied. Mind you, I have to admit, nothing stayed tidy for long.

One of my new friends was Marley, a lovely all-white male, aged, so he informed me, just five months. Unfortunately his owner brought him to Amazonia because he was deaf, and she could not cope with the idea of him being killed on the road. I could understand her fear, but we cats can be kept indoors as house cats, as long as there is plenty to occupy our paws and brains. We do possess thought processes.

Marley and I have become great mates, playing with the toys that our foster-mum has so kindly provided. We love to run like maniacs in and out of empty litter bags. We like the crackle as we pounce and flatten the bags.

By the way, I have neglected to describe myself. I am an all-black, domestic, short-haired cat.

My foster-mum dropped a minuscule amount of liquid on my neck, and my pals told me it was to kill any horrible fleas. I was also given a worming powder mixed in with my lunch.

Anyway, I must continue describing my other companions.

There are two feral cats here too. One is a black and white domestic, short-haired cat called Tosca. She is very charming and not at all vicious. The other is a grey and white tabby. She is called Rosie. Both have been spayed, which means, so I have been informed, that they cannot have kittens.

However, someone whispered in my tiny black ear that Rosie came into Amazonia pregnant on the 11th of June. On the 13th (a Sunday) she gave birth, but, owing to her youth, she did not have sufficient milk to suckle the four two-inch kittens. My poor foster-mum was so upset, because they were all dead by the Monday. I gather there might have been hope for one, but Rosie lay on the kitten's little body, and that was that. Rosie and Tosca were spayed not long after.

There is a dear elderly female called Molly. She is black and white, and her fur is a little matted. She sleeps most of the time, and eats when she feels inclined. She is no bother to us youngsters.

A week ago, another kitten arrived. He is about four months old. He is a grey tabby with white 'socks', hence his name: Socks.

Socks told me he had been found abandoned in an area similar to the one from which I was rescued. A kind married couple brought him to good old Amazonia.

He is sweet, fun and loveable, and we are great pals too. We share our food dish, and play hard.

We are all cosy in our home down the garden. The sides are open to let in fresh air and sunshine. The radio plays soft music, and we never feel alone.

Ten days ago I was taken to the vet's, to have my vaccination for cat flu and feline enteritis. Ouch! It hurt, but I know it was for my own good health. I need to return in three weeks for the booster. Then I can be rehomed eventually to a loving, respectful family. Then I can build my confidence again with mankind.

Man can be (and often is) so cruel to us four-legged creatures. All we want is love, protection and most of all respect. We cats can be so loyal and affectionate in the right environment.

Well it is the 27th of July. I am still here, but I revel in happiness with my pals. I know that if it had not been for the kindness of the gentleman who saved me, and my foster-mum at Amazonia, I would now be in heaven. Thank you.

Shadowlands
(Our Home at Amazonia)

Oh, what a lovely day! It is raining and very blustery, but we are OK. Our foster-mum has just provided breakfast and cleaned our litter trays. The cattery we are in is named Shadowlands. Our foster-mum had it erected out of her own money in 2004, and it is surprisingly cosy and warm.

I would like to relate our little stories, before I curl up on my fleece bed listening to the radio. It's not a bad life really.

I am Molly, an eight-year-old tortoiseshell, with half a tail – something to do with my genes, I believe.

My owner brought me to Shadowlands in May 2008. He, in his wisdom, decided to emigrate to Adelaide, Australia, with his family. I vaguely remember him saying to our foster-mum, "She is used to being in a cattery for periods of time." So here I am.

I do have companions. One is Snowy. As her name implies, she is all white, apart from freckles around

her mouth. Snowy is huge (overweight, I would say) whereas I am quite slim.

Snowy is only one and a half years old, but unfortunately she has a temper. She does not hold back with her claws if I go too near her. Of course, I retaliate, but then I walk away to sulk.

Lately Snowy has calmed down, ever since two lovely female tabbies came in. They are called Mary Jane (mum) and Jasmine (daughter). Mary Jane is eight years old and Jasmine is a year younger. They are very sweet, and they settled in pretty quickly.

Our foster-mum has provided us with small cloth houses, under the chair and in the actual bedroom area, so that we can have our privacy. There is room to move around and play if we are in the mood. There is also a radio. We have comfy beds, and heat pads are provided during the winter months. We have a good view of a bird table, bamboos, a pond with real fish, and a huge cheetah statue.

Jasmine and Mary Jane came in with magnets attached to their collars. It was quite comical when their steel food dish was placed on the floor. The steel was attracted to the collars, and the food dish was dragged around the compartment. Naturally, most of the food was emptied out, so the collars were removed.

Last Thursday afternoon another female came in. She is named Mia – a friendly soul. She has long grey-black fur. She is twelve years old, but our foster-mum does not mind. She will care for us all for as long as necessary: until she is satisfied with a potential owner.

Well, the sun is attempting to poke through the

steely sky. We have been given our lunch, and our litter trays have been cleaned, so now we are settling down at 12.10 for our afternoon siesta. We doze until 4.30 p.m., then – Hooray! – teatime and bedtime. Goodnight to all. We listen to soft night-time music, and the breeze. See you, Mum, in the morning!

Postscript: We in Shadowlands heard through pussy chatter, from the bottom cattery, that on Saturday, the 9th of August 2008, the elderly black and white female, also called Molly, had a stroke. Our foster-mum's son took Molly to the vet, but she did not return. It is very sad.

Pipkins
(My True Story, 2000–2006)

My name is Pipkins. I am a pale-coloured ginger tom. My first owner, a lady, decided in her wisdom to hand me over to a rescue centre in Bristol. The reason was that, although I have been neutered, I was a naughty boy around her 'posh' house.

So, one day I arrived very irate at a home named Amazonia, out in the suburbs of Bristol. I was dutifully placed gently into a relatively comfortable cattery at the bottom of my foster-mum's very wooded garden. My original owner showed no compassion, signed a formality paper and left.

Well, I had a good look around my new home. My foster-mum was exceptionally caring: I had a fleece-lined bed (heated too!), dishes of biscuits, fresh water and toys, and there were photos of previous rescue cats and kittens pinned to the beams. I was not alone. A radio was provided, and the view was good. I could watch the wild birds coming in to feed from the seed trays on the cattery roof, and I saw a young grey

squirrel, which pounced on the nuts provided. The garden plants included lots of conifers, and bamboos – what could be more exotic?

I had visits from a variety of weird potential owners. Some I liked, and some I willingly ignored – especially when the same old query cropped up in the chit-chat: "Does he spray?"

My foster-mum's reply was, "That's the reason Pipkins is here."

Time passed. I was happy. No one bothered me. Sylvia, my foster-mum, cared for me very well. She frequently gave me tuna, and there was always a variety of cat biscuits. She also cleaned my litter tray often. As a result, I never sprayed in the cattery.

I did not find a home for a long time, so one day my foster-mum – bless her! – decided to take me into the bosom of her own home. Gosh! Wasn't I the lucky one?

There were other cats in the house, and their ages ranged from ten to fifteen years. They were a variety of colours and sizes.

Sylvia kept me indoors for over a month, so I would become used to the surroundings and the other cats and not run away.

I have to admit, my temperament was excellent – I never quarrelled or clawed the furniture, though my foster-mum was very lenient about most things.

I became accustomed to sleeping on her bed, close to her face, purring and feeling her hand stroking my soft fur.

At last the month of confinement was over, and I was permitted to go into the garden.

I found the back garden very exciting, with all the variety of wild birds flying in and trees to climb. I hasten to add, I did not catch any wild creatures; I was too amenable.

One day, the lounge window was open, so I hesitatingly made my way to the window sill, sniffed the air, and hopped out rather clumsily on to the wheelie bins close by.

There I met a lovely male tabby called Tigga. He lived two doors down. His owners never bothered with him. He was outside in all winds and weather. My foster-mum would feed him tuna, and he became my play pal.

We would run in and out of the privet hedge and the flower pots, playing chase. My foster-mum would laugh at our antics. No damage was done.

Unfortunately, I still possessed my silly habit of spraying, which annoyed the rest of the family, but Sylvia always sided with me, thank goodness – otherwise I would have been out!

I had an excellent relationship with the other cats, and I was always pleased to see Tigga waiting for me on the wheelie bins to enjoy a good old pussy romp. We never went out on to the road but in any case it was a narrow cul-de-sac so any vehicles had to drive slowly.

I enjoyed my time at Amazonia, but one day I did not feel too well. I ate my tuna and played with Tigga, but then, unusually for me, I went behind the spare-room bed for a rest.

My foster-mum found me on the Sunday morning

at about four o'clock. My little soul had left my body. I knew it would be a dreadful shock for her, but I guess my time had come. I know my foster-mum still has plenty of rescue cats and kittens to care for – and God bless her for that caring attitude.

Postscript: A post-mortem was performed that Sunday morning in September 2006, and a later phone call told me that Pipkins had multiple tumours in his abdomen. He had shown no sign of pain. It was amazing the control he had – never to be forgotten.

La Chambre sous la Cuisine pour les Chats
(The Room under the Kitchen for Cats)

Hello. Let me introduce my companions and myself:

There are four of us in this large room, beneath our foster-mum's kitchen.

My name is Joshua. I am a pedigree cat, and the name of my breed is Turkish Van – not transit van! I am white, with ginger ears and tail, and I have long fur that easily becomes matted. Well, I arrived at Amazonia six weeks ago in a kindly cat trap. I had been wandering the streets locally – in other words, I am a stray. A lady in the area gave me food for a short while, but she decided that I should be caught and taken to a rehoming base. So here I am. The room is large and carpeted, and there are chairs and cat beds aplenty. There is also a radio, tuned to a classical music station, which we all find very soothing.

I have a reputation for being exceptionally mouthy – miaowing loudly, almost Pavarotti-style, hence my nickname now. I am friendly, but inclined to nip people gently around the ankles and fingers. I know I

am gorgeous. If there were a mirror available I would be a genuine Narcissus.

Anyway, I am content. The food is varied and the water is changed regularly, though the litter trays do need flushing more than my foster-mum can keep up with. I whisper, "Sorry, Mum!" but nature has its own way.

My three companions are fine. There are two Siamese females, both thirteen years old. One is named Hannah, and the other, Sheba. They have come from different owners, but they cuddle up together in any one of the beds. They are OK as far as females go.

The other puss is called Susie. She came in today (the 19th). Her owner put her carrier on the floor, opened the flap, and immediately Susie brought up her breakfast. Oh well, another chore for our foster-mum! I guess Susie does not like taxis.

She is fifteen years old – a long-haired tabby. She is a little fiery, but that is to be expected. She was with someone for fifteen years, then plonked in with us rascals. I am sure she will settle – at least, she ate some tuna this morning (the 20th), and she is a little quieter than she was.

She has her own toothpaste and special dental biscuits. It's all right for some, huh?

Our foster-mum will take in cats of any age, to give them a chance of safety, food and warmth. In most cases, the alternative would be the 'sleeping needle' at the vet's. We are lucky and grateful, even if we do make a noise and mess. Miaow, Mum!